Ex Libris
P. M. Dangerfield.

College House, 45, East Street, Faversham, Kent. Faversham 2302.
August 4th 1980.

Lollipops

chosen by
Brian Thompson
illustrated by
Peter Bailey
Quentin Blake
Charles Keeping
and
Barry Wilkinson

Kestrel Books

KESTREL BOOKS
Published by Penguin Books Ltd
Harmondsworth, Middlesex, England

Copyright © 1971 by Longman Group Limited

All rights reserved. No part of this publication may be reproduced, stored in a retrieval system, or transmitted in any form or by any means, electronic, mechanical, photocopying, recording, or otherwise, without the prior permission of the Copyright owner.

Originally published under the Longman Group Limited imprint 1971
Second impression 1973   Third impression 1975
Fourth impression 1979

ISBN 0 7226 5364 6

Printed in Hong Kong by
Wing Tai Cheung Printing Co Ltd

Acknowledgements

We are grateful to the following for permission to reproduce copyright material: Allen Lane, The Penguin Press and Simon & Schuster, Inc. for 'The Sunbeams' by Linda Pidgeon from *Miracles* collected by Richard Lewis; editor's agents and The Bodley Head Ltd for 'There was a small maiden named Maggie' and 'There was a young lady of Spain' from *Limerick Giggles* edited by William Cole; Jonathan Cape Ltd for 'The elephant knocked the ground with a stick' by Adrian Mitchell from *Poems*; Gerald Duckworth & Co Ltd for 'The Dodo' and 'The Elephant' from *Bad Child's Book of Beasts* by Hilaire Belloc; Faber & Faber Ltd and Little, Brown & Co for 'People' from *Laughing Time* by William Jay Smith; author's agents for 'Henry and Mary' from *Collected Poems 1965* by Robert Graves, published by Cassell & Co Ltd; author's agents and Holt, Rinehart Winston Inc for 'Flux' by Carl Sandburg from *Chicago Poems*; Houghton Mifflin Co for 'Grizzly Bear' from *The Children Sing in the Far West* by Mary Austin; Macmillan & Co Ltd for 'The Hamster' by Elizabeth Jennings from *The Secret Brother and Other Poems*; Methuen & Co Ltd for 'Happiness' from *When We Were Very Young* by A. Milne; Nigel Nicolson, literary executor to V. Sackville-West for 'The greater cats with golden eyes'; the author for 'Toucannery' by Jack Prelutsky; the author for 'The Fox Rhyme' by Ian Serraillier; the author for 'Oh, who will wash the tiger's ears' by Shel Silverstein; author's agents, M. B. Yeats and Macmillan & Co Ltd for 'To a Squirrel at Kyle-Na-No' from *The Collected Poems of W. B. Yeats.*

Part One

Contents

Ploffskin, Pluffskin, Pelican jee! *Edward Lear*	1
The Eagle *Alfred, Lord Tennyson*	2
Grey goose and gander	3
I saw eight magpies in a tree	4
Swan, swan, over the sea	6
Little Trotty Wagtail *John Clare*	7
There was an Old Man with a beard *Edward Lear*	8
Three little Tom-tits	9
Little Robin Redbreast sat upon a rail	10
The cock is crowing *William Wordsworth*	11
Riddle me, riddle me ree	12
Toucannery *Jack Prelutsky*	14
The Dodo *Hilaire Belloc*	15
Go to bed first—a golden purse	16

Birds

Ploffskin, Pluffskin, Pelican jee!
We think no birds so happy as we!
Plumpkin, Ploshkin, Pelican jill!
We think so then, and we thought so still!

Edward Lear

The eagle

He clasps the crag with hookèd hands:
Close to the sun in lonely lands,
Ringed with the azure world, he stands.

The wrinkled sea beneath him crawls;
He watches from his mountain walls.
And like a thunderbolt he falls.

Alfred, Lord Tennyson

I saw eight magpies in a tree,
Two for you and six for me:

One for sorrow,

two for mirth,

Three for a wedding,

four for a birth:

Five for England,

six for France,

Seven for a fiddler,

eight for a dance.

Swan, swan, over the sea
Swim, swan, swim.
Swan, swan, back again
Well swum swan.

Little Trotty Wagtail, he went in the rain,

And twittering, tottering sideways, he ne'er got straight again;

He stooped to get a worm, and looked up to get a fly,

And then he flew away ere his feathers they were dry.

John Clare

There was an Old Man with a beard
Who said, "It is just as I feared! –
Two Owls and a Hen, four Larks and a Wren,
Have all built their nests in my beard!"
                                    Edward Lear

Three little Tom-tits
All lost their wits
When first they saw
A pig in fits.

Little Robin Redbreast sat upon a rail;
Niddle naddle went his head,
Wiggle waggle went his tail.

Little Rob Robin,
Where do you live?
Up in yonder wood, sir,
On a hazel twig.

The cock is crowing,
The stream is flowing,
The small birds twitter,
The lake doth glitter,
The green field sleeps in the sun.

The oldest and youngest
Are at work with the strongest:
The cattle are grazing,
Their heads never raising,
There are forty feeding like one!

William Wordsworth

Riddle me, riddle me ree
A hawk sat up in a tree;
And he said to himself said he,
"Oh dear! what a fine bird I be."

The dove says, "Coo
What shall I do?
It's hard, it's hard to keep my two."

"Pooh", says the wren,
"Why, I've got ten
And keep them all like gentlemen."

Toucannery

whatever one toucan can do
is sooner done by toucans two
and three toucans it's very true
can do much more than two can do

and toucans numbering two plus two can
manage more than all the zoo can
in fact there is no toucan who can
do what four or three or two can.

                    Jack Prelutsky

The Dodo used to walk around
And take the sun and air,
The Sun yet warms his native ground –
The Dodo is not there!
That voice which used to squawk and squeak
Is now forever dumb –
Yet may you see his bones and beak
All in the Museum.

Hilaire Belloc

Go to bed first –
A golden purse.

Go to bed second –
A golden pheasant.

Go to bed third –
A golden bird.

Part Two

Contents

Hour after hour *William Jay Smith*	1
Fishes swim in water clear	2
What are little girls made of?	2
What are little boys made of?	3
Come buy my fine apples	4
Hey diddle, dinkety, poppety pet	4
Up the chimney then he goes	5
Here, ladies are cotton	5
There was a young lady of Spain	6
There was an old man and he had nought	7
There was an old person of Brigg *Edward Lear*	8
The Gallant Highwayman *James De Mille*	9
Bobby Shafto's gone to sea	10
Little girl, little girl where have you been?	11
There were three jovial huntsmen	12
There was an old woman	13
The Further Adventures of Simple Simon	14
A little old woman, as I've heard tell	15
Henry was a young king *Robert Graves*	16

People

Hour after hour,
In many places,
People sit,
Making faces.

William Jay Smith

Fishes swim in water clear,
Birds fly up into the air,
Serpents creep along the ground,
Boys and girls run round and round.

What are little girls made of?
What are little girls made of?
Sugar and spice,
And all things nice,
That's what little girls are made of.

What are little boys made of?
What are little boys made of?
Frogs and snails,
And puppy-dogs' tails,
That's what little boys are made of.

"Come buy my fine apples
The old woman cries.
You cannot have better
For eating or pies."

Hey diddle, dinkety, poppety pet,
The merchants of London they wear scarlet,
Silk in the collar, and gold in the hem,
So merrily march the merchant men.

There was a young lady of Spain,
Who couldn't go out in the rain,
 'Cause she'd lent her umbrella
  To Queen Isabella
Who never returned it again.

There was an old man and he had nought,
And robbers came to rob him;

He crept up the chimney pot,
And then they thought they had him;

But he got down the other side,
And so they could not find him;
He ran fourteen miles in fifteen days,
And never looked behind him.

There was an old person of Brigg,
Who purchased no end of a wig;
So that only his nose, and the end of his toes,
Could be seen when he walked about Brigg.

Edward Lear

It was a gallant highwayman
That stopped the Royal Mail;
The ladies shrieked and swooned away
The gentlemen turned pale.

"Forbear," the courteous robber said,
"Your outcries and your curses,
For you can take your lives away
By giving up your purses."

James De Mille

Bobby Shafto's gone to sea,
Silver buckles at his knee;
He'll come back and marry me,
Bonny Bobby Shafto.

Bobby Shafto's bright and fair,
Combing down his yellow hair;
He's my own for ever more,
Bonny Bobby Shafto.

There were three jovial huntsmen
As I have heard them say,
And they would go a-hunting
Upon a summer's day.

All the day they hunted,
And nothing could they find
But a ship a-sailing,
A-sailing with the wind.

One said it was a ship
The other he said nay,
The third said it was a house
With the chimney blown away.

There was an old woman
   called Nothing-at-all,
Who lived in a dwelling exceedingly small;

A man stretched his mouth
   to its utmost extent

And down at one gulp,
   house and old woman went.

Simple Simon went to look
If plums grew on a thistle.
He pricked his fingers very much
Which made poor Simon whistle.

Simon made a great snowball
And brought it in to roast.
He laid it down before the fire
And soon the ball was lost.

Simple Simon went a-fishing
For to catch a whale,
All the water he had got
Was in his mother's pail.

Simple Simon went a-hunting
For to catch a hare.
He rode on a goat about the street
But could not find one there.

A little old woman, as I've heard tell,
Lived near the sea, in a nice little shell;
She was well off, if she wanted her tea —
She'd plenty of water from out of the sea.

Then if for her dinner she had the least wish,
Of course she had nothing to do but to fish;
So, really, this little old woman did well,
As she didn't pay rent for the use of the shell.

Henry was a young king,
   Mary was a queen;
He gave her a snowdrop
   On a stalk of green.

All for his kindness
   And all for his care
She gave him a new-laid egg
   In the garden there.

"Love, can you sing?"
              "I cannot sing."
"Or tell a tale?"
              "Not one I know."
"Then let us play at queen and king
As down the garden walks we go."

Robert Graves

Part Three

Animals

Contents

Higglety, pigglety, pop!
   Samuel Griswold Goodrich   1
There was a small maiden named
   Maggie   2
I am his Highness's dog at Kew
   Alexander Pope   3
Riddle-me, riddle-me rumpty   4
To a squirrel at Kyle-Na-No
   W. B. Yeats   5
The elephant knocked the ground
   with a stick *Adrian Mitchell*   6
The Elephant *Hilaire Belloc*   7
There was an old woman sat spinning   8
If you ever, ever, ever meet
a grizzly bear *Mary Austin*   9
The Hamster *Elizabeth Jennings*   10
Four and twenty tailors
   went to kill a snail   11
If you should meet a crocodile   12
How doth the little crocodile
   Lewis Carroll   13
Aunt was on the garden seat
   Ian Serraillier   14
Oh, who will wash the tiger's ears?
   Shel Silverstein   15
The greater cats with golden eyes
   V. Sackville-West   16

Animals

Higglety, pigglety, pop!
The dog has eaten the mop;

The pig's in a hurry,

The cat's in a flurry,

Higglety, pigglety, pop!

Samuel Griswold Goodrich

There was a small maiden named Maggie,
Whose dog was enormous and shaggy;
   The front end of him
     Looked vicious and grim –
But the tail end was friendly and waggy.

I am his Highness's dog at Kew;
Pray, tell me, sir, whose dog are you?

Alexander Pope

Riddle-me, riddle-me rumpty,
There's a black cat on top of our plum-tree,
I'll bet you a crown
    that I'll soon fetch her down,
Riddle-me, riddle-me rumpty.

See here is a stone; and now it is thrown,
Riddle-me, riddle-me rumpty
Oh, it's just missed her head,
    smashed a window instead,
And the cat's still on top of our plum-tree.

To a squirrel at Kyle-Na-No

Come play with me:
Why should you run
Through the shaking tree
As though I'd a gun
To strike you dead?
When all I would do
Is to scratch your head
And let you go.

W. B. Yeats

The elephant knocked
   the ground with a stick.
He knocked it slow, he knocked it quick.
He knocked it till his trunk turned black –

Then the ground turned round
   and knocked him back.

Adrian Mitchell

When people call this beast to mind
They marvel more and more

At such a little tail behind
So large a trunk before

Hilaire Belloc

There was an old woman sat spinning.

And that's the beginning.

And she had a calf.
And that's half.

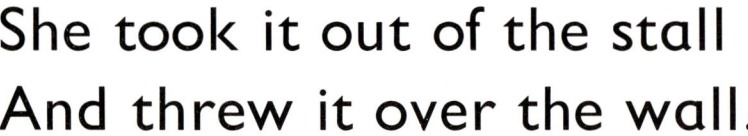

She took it out of the stall
And threw it over the wall.

And that's all.

If you ever, ever, ever meet a grizzly bear,
You must never, never, never ask him *where*
He is going.
Or *what* he is doing;
For if you ever, ever dare
To stop a grizzly bear
You will never meet *another* grizzly bear.

Mary Austin

A hamster by name of Big Cheek
Stored up nuts that would last for a week.
Alas, he ignored
That their being so stored
Made him look the most terrible freak.

Elizabeth Jennings

Four and twenty tailors went to kill a snail.
The best man among them
  dare not touch her tail.
She put out her horns like a little Kyloe Cow
Run, tailors, run or she'll kill you all just now.

If you should meet a crocodile,
Don't take a stick and poke him;
Ignore the welcome in his smile,
Be careful not to stroke him.
For as he sleeps upon the Nile,
He thinner grows and thinner;
And whene'er you meet a crocodile
He's ready for his dinner.

How doth the little crocodile
Improve his shining tail
And pour the waters of the Nile
On every golden scale!

How cheerfully he seems to grin
How neatly spread his claws,
And welcomes little fishes in
With gently smiling jaws.

Lewis Carroll

Aunt was on the garden seat
Enjoying a wee nap and

Along came a fox! teeth
Closed with a snap and

He's running to the woods with her
A-dangle and a-flap and –

Run, uncle, run
And see what has happened!

Ian Serraillier

Oh, who will wash the tiger's ears?
And who will comb his tail?
And who will brush his sharp white teeth?
And who will file his nails?

Oh, Bobby may wash the tiger's ears
And Susy may file his nails
And Lucy may brush his long white teeth
And I'll go down for the mail.

Shel Silverstein

Part Four

Weather

Contents

Whether the weather be cold	1
Sun, Sun do you know	2
Dancy-diddlety-poppety-pin	3
Happiness *A. A. Milne*	4
It's raining, it's pouring	5
Rain rain go away	5
Rain on the green grass	5
One misty moisty morning	6
Doctor Foster	7
White bird featherless	8
Hoddley, poddley, puddle and fogs	9
When the wind is in the east	10
Lily white, rose red	10
The wind has such a rainy sound *Christina Rossetti*	12
Little Billy Tailor	13
When clouds appear like rocks and towers	14
A sunshiney shower	14
Red sky in the morning	14
Purple, yellow, red and green	15
Flux *Carl Sandburg*	16

Weather

Whether the weather be cold
Or whether the weather be hot
We'll weather the weather
Whatever the weather
Whether we like it or not.

Sun, Sun, do you know
You are beams in the flames,
With glow-worms in the light
And bright yellow red
Sharp silver flames
Spinning up,
Like a big block of gold?
The sun is a very magic fellow.

Linda Pidgeon (age 7)

Dancy-diddlety-poppety-pin,
Have a new dress when summer comes in;
  When summer goes out,
  'Tis all worn out,
Dancy-diddlety-poppety-pin.

John had
Great Big
Waterproof
Boots on;
John had a
Great Big
Waterproof
Hat;
John had a
Great Big
Waterproof
Mackintosh —
And that
(said John)
Is
That.

A. A. Milne

It's raining, it's pouring,
The old man's snoring.
He went to bed and bumped his head,
And couldn't get up in the morning.

Rain rain go away,
Come again another day
All the children want to play.

Rain on the green grass
Rain on the tree,
Rain on the housetop
But not on me.

One misty moisty morning
When cloudy was the weather,
There I met an old man
Clothed all in leather;
Clothed all in leather
With cap under his chin.
How do you do, and how do you do
And how do you do again?

Doctor Foster went to Gloucester
In a shower of rain;
He stepped in a puddle,
Right up to his middle,
And never went there again.

White bird featherless
Flew from Paradise
Pitched on the castle wall;

Along came Lord Landless,
Took it up handless

And rode away horseless
 to the King's white hall.

Hoddley, poddley, puddle and fogs
Cats are to marry the poodle dogs;
Cats in blue jackets and dogs in red hats
What will become of the mice and the rats?

The skilful fisherman goes not forth..

When the wind is in the East, it's neither good for man nor beast.

standing in the garden bed. Wind from the South, wind from the

It blows the bait in the fish's mouth.

eleven

The wind has such a rainy sound
Moaning through the town
The sea has such a windy sound, –
Will the ships go down?

The apples in the orchard
Tumble from their tree –
Oh will the ships go down, go down,
In the windy sea?

Christina Rossetti

 twelve

Little Billy Tailor
Gone to be a sailor
His ship's for China bound;
Won't the sea perplex him!
Won't its rolling vex him!
I hope he won't get drowned.

Flux

Sand of the sea runs red

Where the moon slants and wavers.

Sand of the sea runs yellow

Where the sunset reaches and quivers.

Carl Sandburg